PENNY FOR YOUR T

WRITTEN BY PENNY LALLY

Illustrated by Rob Lyttle

For John

Penny Lally

First published in Great Britain 2004 by Rose Farm Publications

Copyright © Penny Lally 2004

ISBN 0-9548505-0-5

Printed in Great Britain by Headland Printers, Penzance, Cornwall

Cover illustration from an original by Gay Sagar-Fenton (the author's mother)

PENNY FOR YOUR THOUGHTS

Poems from Rose Farm

WRITTEN BY PENNY LALLY

Illustrated by Rob Lyttle

Welcome to this book of poems, beautifully set off by Rob Lyttle's atmospheric water-colours. Between them they portray a world which may seem dreamlike to those whose lives are spent in town. But it is real enough, and not always idyllic. The country can be blissful but it can be cruel too, it can tug at your heart, but sometimes break it…

You too could live Penny's life, but only if you don't mind being on the go fifteen hours a day, seven days a week, presenting a cheerful face to paying guests, finding genuine sympathy for those who bring their animals to the pet cemetery she runs with her husband John, having as sure a touch with a new-born puppy as a massive Simmental bull or an unbroken colt; if you can go to county shows and come home with hatfuls of prizes, then quietly mould beautiful heads in clay, as well as feeding, cleaning out and caring for a huge variety of creatures, many of them with two legs – oh and still finding the time to record some of this in verse, as you will see. It's that easy.

Penny has no literary pretensions. She paints what she sees, what she thinks, how she feels, in language as direct as it can be when tackling such themes, from dawn to night, from death to canaries. She takes you by the hand and leads you through the year in her eyes, with the clear light of a Cornish morning.

Penny has also been my sister all my life. We are as different as this and that, but we love many of the same things, from Nature to Manchester United. She is admittedly crazy, but her feet are firmly rooted in her native soil, she doesn't miss much, and she's not a bad soul. I'm proud of her. Besides she's got Sky, so I need to keep on her right side…

Open your eyes, your mind and heart and enjoy.

Mike Sagar-Fenton

EARLY MORNING

Warm sun, wet grass, butterflies on blackberries
Busy morning bees
Crowing cockerels, distant crying calves
Wisps of early mist snaking, serpent-like
Through the valley trees
Contented cattle chewing cud and basking in golden light.
Cool shadowy lane
Sparkling dew drops with million rainbows
A faithful dog beside.
Clear, clean autumn air sharp in your nostrils
Footprints track in the dewy grass, foxy smells,
Rabbits scuttling to ground
Soaring seagulls, swooping swallows chattering.
Silver, silent aircraft overhead
Grazing sheep, cool and happy
Horses flicking flies with swishing tails
– Inquisitive, beautiful, shining.
The silence is deafening – no wind
Just busy beasts all shapes and sizes pleased
To be alive on such a day
WHO WILL SPOIL IT?
Man-machines-telephones-traffic
Deadlines- stress-worry
Unaware what is always there, peaceful, free
– Birds and beasts, unflustered
Unimpressed with material things.
Mother Earth, caring, providing, solid
– AMAZING.

LUNAR LIGHT SHOW

In the theatre in the sky
The moon put on a show
The dark blue velvet curtains
Obscured the golden glow

The audience of stars
With patience, quietly shone.
To see this lunar spectacle –
Would we wait for long?

The velvet curtains drew aside
Revealing lacy net…
The leading actress in the role
Was not ready yet!

A tantalizing orange glow
Tempted straining eyes
The 'net' disbursed, the audience gasped
At the magic of the skies

A diamond sparkle edged the sphere
Which now was autumn red,
The diamond turned to crescent
As the moon her shadow shed

The clouds, like 'stripper's' fans,
Teased us with the view.
The stars and I were privileged
To watch in morning dew

And for the grand finale
A 'shooting star' fell past
Another special memory
Which will ever last.

EARLY MORNING RIDE

The cherry blossom on the tree
The shimmering sunlight on the sea
A skylark singing overhead
Most sleepy people still in bed
The pink of early morning sky
A cuckoo, silent, flying by
A hedge of egg-yolk yellow gorse
Surround me on my happy horse.
Just him and me in morning air
Our time – alone – no one can share.
High in blue sky, clear, above
Two planes cross trails in X kiss of love,
Their passengers all packed in tight
Experiencing a long, dull flight,
No bird-song there, just noise and chat –
Where I am, there's no sound like that
Just metal shoes on road of tar
Break the silence where we are
A vixen warmed by rising sun
Wanders home, her hunting done
Back to her Earth where cubs await
Chattering in expectant state.
A cockerel crows in farmyard near,
A cheery morning voice to hear,

Telling hens, with all his heart,
Another day is about to start.
Over distant sea and sky
The seagulls soar, and wheel and cry.
Which ever way I look, I see
A glorious vista just for me
The countryside in spring attire
The rising sun, a ball of fire
Warming grass of luscious green
Shining there so fresh and clean,
It waits for cows of black and white
Who sleep on straw, in sheds, at night.
As horse and I progress along
The stirring world begins to throng
Our time, alone, is soon to end.
So home we go me and my friend
Of this new day – we've had the best
Now we can leave it to the rest
While they rush madly on their way.
Tomorrow is another day
I can have, if early rise
There never was a better prize.
Who needs money? This is free!
To have, each day, my horse and me.

BRIAN

Brian is my canary
His cage is near my sink
And when I do the washing up
He likes a chat – I think.
His head cocks at an angle
His beady eyes are bright
This feathered yellow person
Is such a sunny sight.
He hops from perch to perch
Or chirps when on his swing
And when he hears the Hoover
Sings as loud as he can sing.
When the cat jumps on the side
Brian shouts a special cry
And warns, "That feline menace
Would like to see me die!"
This little bird is jolly
And chatty in his way
It is a joy to watch him
And speak with him each day.

CAT BY THE FIRE

What is it that a cat sees?
Why does he sit and stare?
Who is it in those dancing flames?
Maybe he knows someone there
Curled up on a hearth rug
Relaxing without care
What does he think – who does he see?
Why does he sit and stare?

MOUNTS BAY MORNING

Early Morning Sea like molten silver in the Bay
"The Mount" a silhouette against the sun
Waves were sighing sweetly, as they gently kissed the shore
Another lovely day had just begun.

Delighted dogs ran fast and free across the rippled sand
Seagulls bobbed contentedly close by
Only flying most begrudgingly, disturbed by chasing hounds,
Without effort, high into a cloudless sky.

The night train was arriving on the railway track besides
The ever-changing tide and shifting sands.
The line it goes no further now, the terminus is reached
This station is the last one, or first one in the land.

The disembarking passengers, hurried home, or off to work
The stirring town awake for morning shifts
But all was calm and peaceful on this lazy morning beach
Its beauty just one more of nature's gifts.

RUSH HOUR

Every morning soon after it's light
The commuter starlings fly into sight
These 'Business Birds' in suits so neat
Fill the sky, the dawn to greet.
Where have they come from – far or near?
They fly with purpose, that is clear.
The 'whoosh' of their wings as they pass in a cloud
Makes a breeze in the air from this fluttering crowd
Where are they going? – we'll never know
But they'll be back tomorrow for the morning show.

TRAIN JOURNEY

I'm sitting here upon this train
My face close to the window pane
Starting out into the dawn
Watching 'Thursday' being born.

The sky is pink and green and grey
It's going to be a lovely day
A frosty mist in valleys lie
Some cattle graze as we speed by

Lambs, on their mothers, leap and play
A rabbit, startled, runs away.
The farmhouse lights are twinkling bright
A day begins, now ends the night

The sun is climbing in the sky
Some pigeons in a circle fly
A farmer tending to his stock
Is checking all his woolly flock

And now we pass through factory yards
And houses built like packs of cards
Then – out into the countryside
Where swans on glassy water glide.

A workman saws up wood for logs
Some children exercise their dogs
And off to work the people drive
Like bees emerging from a hive

The train cuts through the morning air
Rushing past without a care
Grinding on the rails of steel
Keeping on an even keel

It transports us from place to place
With our belongings in a case
We sit and stare, or read, or write
As day begins to catch up night.

MY AGA

Mother AGA sitting there
It's cold outside, why should we care?
The room is warm and all is grand
Next to this heat we love to stand
Or learn or sit, like dog or cat –
The perfect comfort feeling, that.

But, once a year, we dread the date
To turn the AGA off we hate.
The corpse of red enamel lies,
No living sound, no gentle sighs
A block of cold you cannot touch
We miss our AGA very much

No simmering kettle on the hob –
Must use electric for that job.
A chill creeps slowly round the place
But wait – who is that smiling face
The AGA KHAN (or doctor) comes
To restore the heat for warming 'bums'
Replacing wicks and checking parts
Bringing joy to all our hearts

And slowly, slowly life returns
As mother AGA's blue flame burns
She sits and watches, night and day.
Her welcome warmth is here to stay.

BLOT

'Blot' is at the window –
It must be going to rain
He'll stay in for a while –
Then go out once again.
He has a busy life
Checking all his haunts,
I wonder where he goes
On his daily jaunts.

He is concentrating now
His ablutions must be done
Cleaning all his fur
With his rasping tongue
Then…a little sleep
Somewhere comfortable and warm
It could be by the AGA
Or on the settee arm
Or even on the table
Where I'm trying to write
What 'Blot' wants – he will have
It's pointless putting up a fight.

When he wants his food
You'll be aware,
Wherever you are
He'll be there,
Underfoot and in the way,
Until he's fed
That's where he'll stay.

He is an independent cat
Content, I am quite sure of that
His presence fills the room he's in
He is quiet, none of that feline 'din'.

He is comfortable in black and white
When he's about, the house feels right.
King of his castle, that's for sure.
'Blot' the cat found on the moor.

PATIOS AND PAVING STONES

Patios and paving stones –
Plastic garden chairs –
Flowerpots and borders
A hedge which neighbours share
Swimming pools and sheds –
Decking – flowering shrubs
Paths of coloured gravel
Bedding plants in tubs.
Some are neat and tidy
Others are a mess
And where some start and finish
You really have to guess!
Occasionally a broken car
And rubbish strewn in piles
The English back gardens
Have a dozen different styles
To view them from the train
Is a way to pass the time,
Fun on the longest journey
On a rumbling railway line
Each one a different symbol
Of the characters inside
I like to think, 'What are they like?'
And what sort of life they lead
Each one a mental picture
As we travel past at speed.

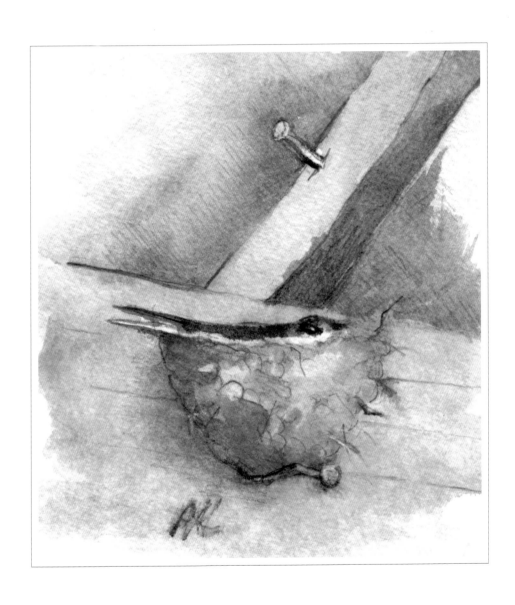

THE BEECH GROVE

Majestic, magnificent, queen of the trees
High on the hill that everyone sees
Protected by 'courtiers', elegant, proud
So near, yet so far, away from the crowd
Imposing, yet welcoming landmark on high
The tops of the branches reaching the sky
Silhouette ever changing in winter or spring
Yet solid and steady, they make your heart sing
Ancient and magic, wise old beech trees
Healing, inspiring, cathedrals are these
Shelter for sheep and horses and birds
Shady in summer for the fly bothered herds
Of cattle, who graze at the feet of the queen
Dressed in her cloak of beautiful green
She's moody yet gracious in her lofty abode
Unmoved by the hurrying cars on the road
With drivers so stressed by the traffic ahead
Or tired when their eyelids are feeling like lead
…If they looked, and paid homage to beauty and grace
They would feel a broad smile spreading over their face
For that sight, so serene, joining earth to the sky
Can rid you of worry and replace with a sigh

FIRST SWALLOW OF SPRING

Today I saw a swallow
Skimming low across the ground
After flying here from Africa
This tiny farm he's found
He is doing some repairs
On the nest he used last year
He liked it so much then
He's going to stay round here.
His wife, she is preparing
For the brood she's going to lay
When hatched, they will need feeding
Every minute of the day.
From their elevated viewpoint
In a stable warm and dry
They will raise their little family
As the world, them, passes by.

We think we are so clever
With computers, cars and planes,
But, just imagine setting off
To fly through winds and rain
To a speck upon a map
So many miles away
And knowing, without telling, that
Till Autumn you will stay
Then off with your new family
You'll fly from whence you came.
Without these chattering characters
Spring would never be the same.

DAIRY COW

Eat, sleep, drink
Through the parlour twice a day
Eat, sleep, drink
I laze the summer days away
Eat, sleep, strain
When my calf is nearly born
Eat, sleep, bellow
When maternal ties are torn
Eat, sleep, shelter
When cold rain soaks my skin
Eat, sleep, comfort
Inside the shed I'm wintered in
Eat, sleep, drink
As the the litres flow each day
Eat, sleep, drink
As my short life slides away
Eat, sleep, drink
How I grace each field of green
Eat, sleep, drink
A contented, peaceful scene
So eat, sleep, drink
That white gold I supply
For I've given you my all
During my life, – then I will die

PACKAGES

What do we do with paper
A present is wrapped in
We say "How very pretty"
And put it in the bin.
But we will keep the gift inside forever.

What happens to the bottle
That contained a vintage port
We put it in a bottle bank
For someone else to sort
But we don't forget each smooth and memorable sip.

We discarded lovely packaging
That held our favourite scent
And threw it with the rubbish
Not caring where it went.
But we can still recall that charming smell.

What happens to our bodies
When life comes to a close
We bury or cremate them
Like old and worn out clothes
But we never will destroy the spirit kept inside.

Emerging from its chrysalis
For which it has no need
Like a butterfly, just flies away
A miracle indeed
But even though we may not see it, we know it's still around…

HEDGEROW FASHIONS

The Foxglove models
Sway gaily in the breeze
They move with stately elegance
Their audience to please

The crowds of cheerful campions,
Their dresses fresh and new
Compliment the bluebells
In a sea of pink and blue

The music at this fashion show
Is provided by the birds
The blackbird and the chaffinch
Write the songs which have no words

The audience, wild garlic
In abundance watch with glee
The ferns are the photographers
For the hedgerow press to see

The buttercups like spotlights
Shine golden in the green
Of leafy carpet – wall to wall,
In this springtime fashion scene.

The sun and sky, a backdrop
For this occasion, staged so well
By: Spring Promotions – Cornish style
This beauteous scene to sell

So many people miss this
When in flashy cars drive by
Caught up with daily problems
It makes me wonder why?

Just stop and look and listen –
Take time to see what's there
It is free for each and everyone
So miss it – if you dare!

MID-SUMMER DREAM

I want to be free like the wind
To blow, where I choose, when I wish
To play in the sea, with a dolphin
Not to be part of a shoal of fish.
I want to fly high like a buzzard
Away from the crowds in their cars
I want to roam free like a leopard
Sleeping out under the stars.
I want to sing just like a blackbird
And treat everyone to a tune
To drift along with the clouds
Or sit quietly and look at the moon
But – I'd better get on with the breakfasts
And put these thoughts out of my head
Just go and be pleasant to visitors
And wash up their dishes instead!

ECLIPSE

The sun and the moon were to marry
The arrangements were going as planned
The time at eleven on a Wednesday
They would appear hand in hand.

The sky was to 'give them away'
The birds' song had been well rehearsed
For a congregation of millions
This wedding, a definite first

The tensions were gradually building
Everyone had to be there
An occasion like this was so special
A time we all had to share

The 'reception' a joyous event
Would suit many a different taste
Whether Pagan or Pope would feel a new hope
As the 'shadow' across the world raced.

The ushers, who were clouds in the sky
Decided the moon bride was shy
So they gathered around to prevent us a view
Of this 'moment' way up in the sky.

But they could not obscure the feelings
As the union of Sun God took place.
The darkness, the silence, the Reverence,
The wonder, on everyone's face

The gloom when a white bird appeared
A seagull flew high overhead
Calling as seagulls do
Proclaiming the 'couple' had wed.

As the shadow of love slipped away
And a strange light returned to the ground
A cock crowed to welcome the day back
We hugged those who gathered around

There was an incredible closeness
We were all filled with joyful relief
That the wedding of moon and of sun
Had happened in a moment so brief.

The powerful Sun had returned
Giving warmth and light to us here
Without him, we would be NOTHING
In a cold world of darkness and fear

The moon, she went back to her Boudoir
The Sun carried on in his way
We 'toasted' the brand new beginnings
We all felt that had started that day.

SPIRIT GUIDES

Jewelled stars like freckles
On the face of midnight sky
The moon, as amber smile
Brightly shines down from on high
The wispy clouds like Angel hair
Drift around in space
The gentle breeze you feel
Like 'breath' upon your face
The Universe is living
Although we cannot see
So many different Spirits
Delighted to be free.
Each one is there to help us
Whilst we're tethered to the Earth
To love us and to guide to us
From the moment of our birth.
So quietly ask your 'helper'
As you struggle on your way
To deal with each experience
You come across today.

SAD ANNIVERSARY

Today my friend I light a flame
And in its glow I see your name
This date, you left the earthly world
And flew with angels wings unfurled
Beyond the clouds and highest peak
Beyond the empty moors so bleak
Beyond the ever stirring sea
So very, very far from me.
Yet, never absent from my mind
Your happy face and thoughts so kind.
I know you're with me when I need
Your helping hand to take a lead.
And when that owl sits in the tree
Her beady eyes look down on me,
I know it's you, a handsome bird
Rarely seen, but often heard
In the still and starry night
Travelling low in silent flight
Then I know you're here, close by
My friend and spirit in the sky.

SEPTEMBER

The berries are red on the trees
There's a "bite" in the fresh morning breeze
The swallows have all gone away
The sun gets up later each day.
The harvest is mostly all done
The visiting children have gone
Back home, to prepare for their school.
The evenings are short and quite cool.
The nine-carrot moon lights the sky
Large and smiling at me from on high
Gentle September is here
August has gone, how I cheer.

ROSE FARM ON NOVEMBER NIGHT

The sun sets, pink, behind church tower
The heavens send another shower.
Animals in deep straw beds
Eat their food, in wooden sheds
All dry and warm as darkness falls
Safe behind their stable walls.

Then – in I go to house so warm
The centre of this little farm
The fires crackle in the hearth
The clock ticks on for all it's worth
All is restful in this place
There's no more need to rush and race
Absorb this peace, breathe in the calm
So safe in here away from harm
From stormy winds and rain I'm freed
A quiet time – so rare indeed
Just fires of wood and chiming clock
This house is solid on a rock
Its arms of love surround your soul
You feel secure and in control
Renewed, recharged, you break the spell
Responding to the ringing bell –
Then carry on with evening chores
(Although they are in, behind closed doors)
But all the time through noise and chatter
Telephone and general clatter
This house remains, a friendly place
The smile of care upon its face
As it has been for centuries past
Where there's love, these feelings last.

NEW MOON

The moon was as new as moon could be
The bats were swooping low and free
The sky was sort of a greyish blue
With groups of clouds in a darker hue
A grumble in the heights of a Jumbo Jet
On the way somewhere, but not there yet.

A WINTER'S AFTERNOON

On an afternoon like this, where I'd like to be
Is sitting by an open fire, drinking cups of tea
Eating toast and honey or sandwiches and cake
And not thinking once, "How fattening", with every bite I take!
The tea would be in pretty cups, elegant and thin
The sandwiches, quite delicate, with assorted fillings in
The cakes, set on a cake stand, with doilies to protect
The antique painted china – "mmmmm", which one should I select?
This experience would be cosy, with friends to share the treat,
Unhurried and relaxing, with delicious things to eat.
The wind would blow its heart out and rattle all the doors
And rain pour down the windows, we've seen it all before.
We would sit for ages, as the work had all been done
And chat on many subjects ---------"Shall I have another bun?".

EVENING WALKIES

The sky draws her curtains on the day
And lights a million candles which flicker brightly
Each one for a spirit remembered.
Blackbirds tell their bedtime stories.
Nature's shifts are changing, some settle down
Some stretch and wake
The silence is so noisy with unseen business.
The dogs trot beside, their nails clicking on the road surface
Their noses twitching with evening scents.
Each house we pass has a warm glow from a window
Cosy – familiar – safe…
Save one – empty – lonely, full of memories, ghostly.
Its walls like arms, longing to embrace new friends –
No Christmas lights in there.
A blaze of headlights and a metal capsule of revving engine
Shatter our peaceful walk as the driver hurries home.
There is a frosty feel to the evening air
We bid goodnight and return to the warmth and comfort of our home –
The dogs curl up and sleep once more.

THE MOON JUDGE

Presiding over inky sky
The moon, in judgement, sits on high
His jury, sparkling, gather round
Twinkling, far above the ground.
The case in question, could be you
The jury ponder, what to do.
The moon, he frowns with puzzled brow
The evening star his clerk for now.
The court recess behind a cloud
The accused awaits with head bowed
A gold edged cloud moves swiftly by
Revealing moon, a judgement nigh
The prisoner, speechless, stands in fear
The sentence passed about to hear
THE PUNISHMENT: From this day forth
To watch the skies form south to north
And look at each and every star
Then realise how small you are-
The merest blink in endless time
A single grape in vat of wine
Enjoy each precious breath you take,
The highest mountain, deepest lake –
The smallest bird, the biggest beast,
On natures wonder you will feast
Absorb the sun, observe the green,
Remember beauty that you've seen
Miss nothing round you – every day.
You're never sure how long your stay
On this planet we call Earth-
Treasure time for all it's worth.

The prisoner listened with a sigh
Receiving sentence from the sky
Reflecting- this is not so bad,
From this day on I will be glad
To be alive, with eyes to see
And ears to hear, and just to be
Surrounded by such lovely things
The poorest are as rich as kings.

So thank you Moon, your golden face
Is smiling in your lofty place.
The jury can retire to bed
The judgement passed, the sentence read.

Here endeth yet another day
The sun is still quite far away
Deciding – shine or not to shine…..
Shall the day be dull or fine?
We shall not know till early morn.
Now tiredness creeps on with a yawn,
So off to bed for welcome sleep-
To the moon my promise keep.

CHRISTMAS

Christmas has gone once again
The rubbish is filling the bin
A horrified glance in the mirror
Sends us scurrying down to the gym

In a flurry of sweat, toil and trainers
As we desperately try to loose weight
Working muscles we long had forgotten
Regretting the food that we ate.

Some people decide to go jogging
Others just walk their dogs…FAST!
The nuts and the chocolate are eaten
The fridge is quite empty, as last.

The bed in the spare room is re-made
It returns to be tidy once more
The last guest has kissed us "goodbye"
As we stand waving at the front door.

The decorations are back in the loft
Each Christmas card now put away
Spring is just round the corner
As the sun stays up longer each day.

A sense of relief is returning
At the thought of an evening at home
Of being entirely unsociable
And sitting, in silence, alone.

Much as we all love our Christmas
And look forward to times of good cheer
Thank Goodness, for the sake of our sanity
That it only comes round once a year!

PROPERTY

A house is just a pile of bricks
Tiles, wood and cement
It is not our forever
Like time, it's only lent

A house can be a castle
Or just a cardboard box
A tunnel in the earth
Is a house to mother fox
It could be made of twigs
Lined with feathers in a tree
Or mud under the eaves
If a swallow you should be
Some houses, they are made of ice
And some are shacks of tin
A house is built for shelter
And to raise a family in

But a house becomes a home
When there's love and warmth inside
Where you welcome friends and family
And care for it with pride
No matter what it looks like
If it's comfortable and warm
And when you close that door
You feel safe from any harm

The countryside is constant
Its beauty there to see
No one really owns it
It is free for you and me
We can breath in all its fragrance
And feel the seasons change
And we'll let Mother Nature
All the colours rearrange

NIGHT

See the moon, touch the stars.
Feel the magic where you are
Wear the moonlight – how it glows
Embrace the breeze that softly blows
Smell the earth so rich and dark
Where your footprints make a mask
Hear the silence of the night
Look up and see the heavenly sight.
A shooting star streaks earthward bound,
Make a wish but not a sound.
Are there Angels in the sky
Looking after you and I
Are our loved ones' 'spirits' there
Free as eagles in the air?
We are never lonely when alone
'They' are not here but never gone.
Enrich your soul – breath in deep
The cool night air – its secrets keep.

SNAILS' PLACE

How nice to be snail
Worries have they few
No need to go house hunting
You just carry it with you.
No worries with a mortgage,
Property boom or bust,
No housework to be done
No polishing, no dust.
No furniture, no carpets,
No beds to make each day
Just when you're out
Your are at home,
And where you go, you stay!

WORT IS DEAD

Life is so uncertain
A fragile thread between two worlds
One minute all is well
The next a deathly cloud unfurls
It gathers in a gloom
And surrounds your aching heart
Like some dreadful dream
In which you have a part.
That helpless frantic feeling
Is replaced by emptiness
A numbing desperation
Your world crumbling in a mess.

He's dead now, no more pain
Buried deep in earthy ground
But Oh! How I will miss him
I loved having him around
A joyful cheeky character
With flowing tail and mane
I really can't believe I won't see him again!
Yet I will, inside my head
That pony-solid-hairy-black.
The Gods may have taken him
– They can't take my memories back

TWO SPIRITS

Two spirits free as air
Set off on wings of time
From West and East they came travelling with the dawn,
To meet somewhere in time.
And when they met,
An ember of passion began to glow in the fireplace of this life.
The glow became a flame
And the spirits, like moths, fluttered and danced around this
crimson flame.
They touched and laughed
And travelled in a bubble of endless time
Floating without a care, caressing, entwined in emotions,
Simmering with this lusty flame –
And then as quickly as the spirits met
The bubble burst, the spirits released
To West and East returned one day to meet again
Who knows when or where?

I WISH

We live in a world full of dreams
Of 'if' and 'maybe' and 'when'
Of 'imagine, just how it would be
If time were to come round again'
Of 'one day this is what I would do'
Perfection is there to achieve
Through it seems always just out of reach.
The requirement – that you must believe

What you wish for is yours if you try
Just focus your thoughts on the aim,
The amount of effort – your choice,
The journey is not without pain
The pleasure is the struggle towards,
The anticipation you feel
The wanting and hoping involved in the turn of that wishing wheel.